101 TIPS FOR STAYING YOUNG AND FOOLISH

MATTHEW BURGESS

National Library of Australia Cataloguing-in-Publication entry

Title: 101 Tips for Staying Young and Foolish / Matthew Burgess;
Book Design by Ocean Reeve Publishing and Dedicated Book Services

ISBN: 978-1-925406-96-2 (paperback)

Subjects: Burgess, Matthew.
View Legal (Firm)
Legal services—Australia.
Finance, Personal—Australia.
Assets (Accounting)—Australia.
Tax planning—Australia.
Estate planning—Australia.

Other Creators/Contributors: Book Design by Ocean Reeve Publishing and Dedicated Book Services

Published by D & M Fancy Pastry in 2018
Typefaces: Myriad Pro

100%
YOU
London
Paris
Berlin
Moscow
Beijing
Tokyo
Sydney
Los Angeles
New York
1/5/35
B1G1
Google
FREE
And; not or
1/1/90
7/11/4

Foreword

Since the early 2000s, I have had the opportunity to work for many incredibly successful and inspirational people, including a significant percentage of the members of the various 'Rich Lists'. My roles have varied widely however, ultimately, have always involved helping people achieve a goal or vision that is part of their life's work.

Like most lawyers, I have had others attach labels to me over the years, including:

- **a.** the baby-faced assassin
- **b.** the lawyer to get when you don't want to deal with a lawyer
- **c.** the 'www' (why the wealthy win) guy.

Undoubtedly there have been many other labels that, even if I knew of them, they would probably not be printable.

Someone, who never appeared on any list, coined the one that has meant the most to me.

She was a small business operator and we helped to ensure she had a structure that allowed her to survive and ultimately prosper during a difficult start-up phase. Her label for what I do is 'The dream enabler' and that is the theme and title of one of my books.

As set out in the foreword to 'The Dream Enabler', for as long as I can remember, the obsessive study of great thinkers has been my favourite pastime.

One aspect of this has been my evolving approach to 'common placing'—that is, the constant collection and ordering of the ideas of others.

Common placing has evolved, for me, from simply hoarding as many of my favourite books as possible, to cataloguing separately my favourite extracts, re-cataloguing extracts into disciplines and themes and to summarising the extracts into a centralised, personal 'bible' loosely titled 'brain food'.

Undoubtedly, everyone has their own learning style.

Successful entrepreneurs generally embrace one or more of the following concepts:

1. You can only join the dots with hindsight.
2. Actively creating serendipity is important.
3. Fail fast.
4. Deliver a 'MVP'—i.e. a minimum viable product, and then iterate and iterate again.
5. Embrace 'loose-tight' thinking.

The Reference Guide, sets out much of the content that for me leverages each of the above concepts and in turn inspired me to write The Dream Enabler. In particular the key concepts in the Reference Guide I explored were:

1. '101 Tips for staying young and foolish'
2. Quotes to note
3. Bibliography

The '101 tips for staying young and foolish' section is a play on a famous Steve Jobs quote 'stay hungry; stay foolish'. The creation of the table of 101 tips in the Reference Guide was largely as a result of my disciplined common placing over many years.

In particular, each of the businesses I have founded has been heavily influenced by an array of thinkers. The capturing of the key messages of those thinkers that have been most relevant for our various business interests saw the creation of many principles, stories and tips over an extended period of time.

The reason for using the word 'young' instead of 'hungry' is that it better captures the interpretation of the quote that resonates most with me; that is 'stay young' = maintain high levels of energy and enthusiasm; 'stay foolish' = ensure a beginners mindset is maintained as much as possible.

All of the material in the Reference Guide ultimately then evolved, with thanks again to common placing, into the following nine key attributes explored in The Dream Enabler, namely:

The three 'P's	The three 'I's	The three 'L's
1. passion	**4.** incubate	**7.** law
2. persistence	**5.** inspire	**8.** learning
3. purpose	**6.** invest	**9.** leverage

In addition to The Dream Enabler book, the material in the Reference Guide has helped create The Dream Enabler Workbook and now this book—101 Tips for Staying Young and Foolish.

The Workbook is designed to provide a catalyst, or starting point, for your personal journey in each of the 9 attributes explored in The Dream Enabler.

While it is a companion to the book, there is certainly no reason that you need have read The Dream Enabler before exploring the Reference Guide or the Workbook.

This said, in areas where you are wanting to deepen your understanding about particular concepts, the comparative chapter in The Dream Enabler will provide the foundation for further learning.

My hope for this book, the Reference Guide, the Workbook and ultimately The Dream Enabler is that it facilitates your personal focused, common placing and that in turn provides the foundation for your continued learning and realising of your dreams.

“The preferred due date on time turnarounds if not today, is yesterday”

Habitually, anyone we service will want things returned as fast as possible, and totally correct.

85%
Don't forget
to cal Thomas
098-764-4318

“Rocks first time; every time”

Every day should start with completion of your hardest, biggest and most important task – all other relevant tasks will magically still get done, so long as this approach is taken.

“Measure twice, cut once”

In all of our work, preparation is twice as important as doing.

“Allow equal time for delivery of first cut to final delivery”

If a task is being promised to a customer within 10 days, the first completed draft should be provided to the reviewer within the first 5 days. It will always take time for the various iterations following this first review, and as a courtesy, the amount of time allowed for that should be equal to the amount of time that was taken to produce the first cut.

“Parkinson’s Law”

This concept is one that has been proven countless times across many industries, particularly in the professional services firms that use time billing. The basic theme is that every task will expand to the maximum available duration. This causes significant risks and stress that should be avoided at all costs, and is part of the reason why the rock concept is so critical.

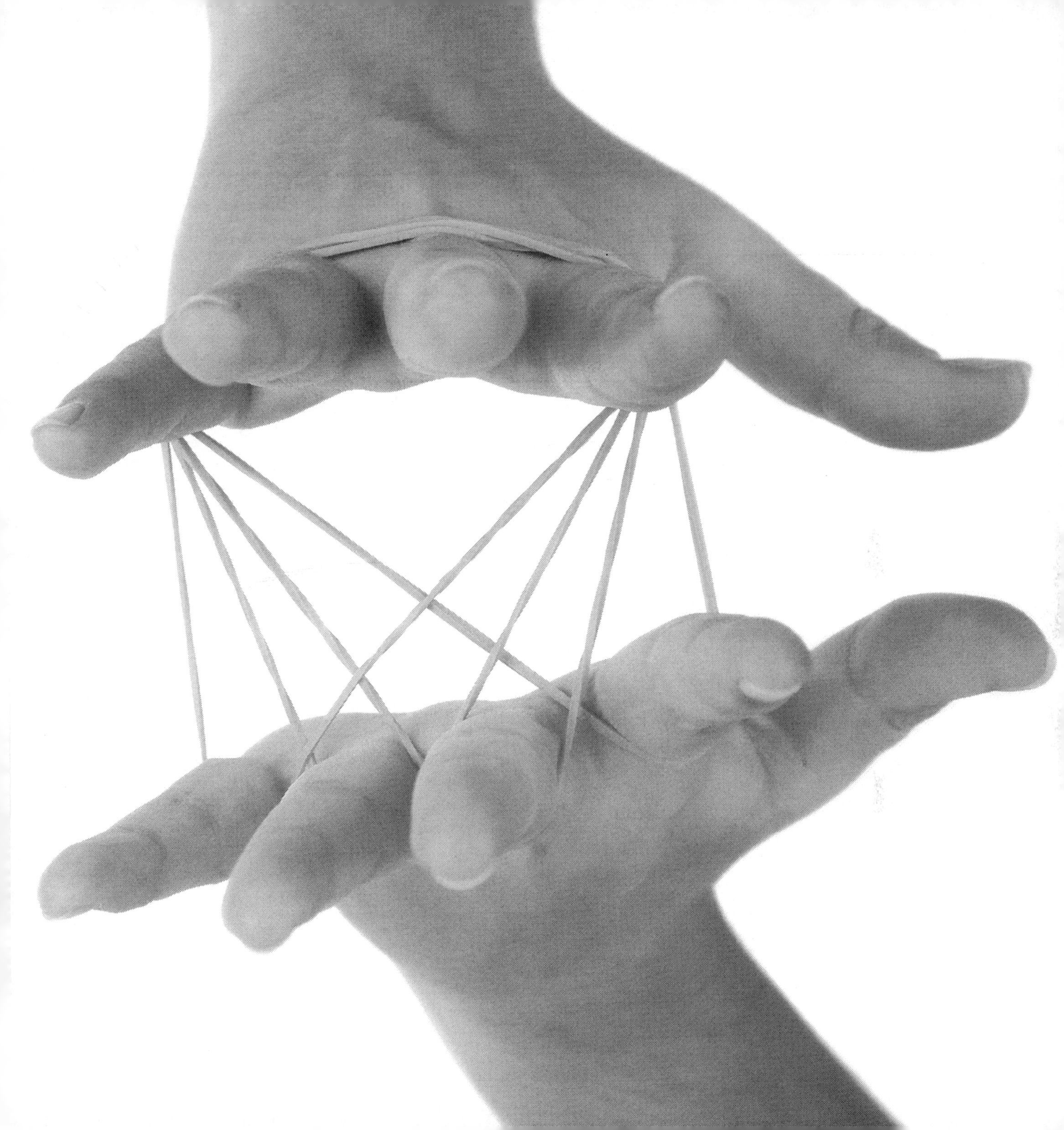

“Price is what you pay … ”

… and value is what you get.

This is one of Warren Buffett’s most famous quotes. In combination with a number of other themes in this book, it explains why we only assist customers on a pre-agreed scope of work with upfront guaranteed fixed pricing.

Price
890.00
Baht

“Murphy’s Law”

Everything that can go wrong will go wrong.

DE L'OUEST
721

“Baker’s Law”

Ron Baker is a mentor for many businesses – he has written numerous books on pricing and also developed what he calls Baker’s Law. Essentially, this means that bad customers drive out good customers because the heavy investment in them distracts us from what is important.

“100% is easy, 99% is hard”

As soon as there are exceptions to any rule, the rule becomes virtually worthless. In other words, it is far easier to do something 100% of the time rather than any percentage less than that because any percentage less requires deep thought as to whether it is truly an exception to the rule.

100%

“UPOD”

Under promise over deliver – whenever communicating with other team members, customers and referral sources, particularly in relation to time turnarounds, it is vital to take ownership of ensuring that a promise is understated and then do everything within your power to over deliver on the promise made.

“Less is more”

Jobs, among many others, is famous for understanding that a key to success in any area is making things as simple as possible; although not simpler (Einstein).

“Never I”

We are a customer centric organisation. Emails and letters that have every sentence starting with ‘I’ are not customer centric – indeed, it is preferable to never start any sentence with an ‘I’.

YOU

“Intraday communication”

A business is founded on constant service delivery performance. Customers expect they are the only people in our lives, and we should therefore do whatever it takes, either directly or via other members of the team, to respond to every phone call and email intraday, even if it means outside 'normal' hours.

London
Paris
Berlin
Moscow
Beijing
Tokyo
Sydney
Los Angeles
New York

“ATM is the answer ”

ATM stands for AutoTextMe. It is the tool that allows us to send emails that are pre-settled virtually instantaneously. In an ideal world, all aspects of communication in our business would be centralised in an ATM. Before then, we should simply use it as often as possible.

“The 3 step work test”

The ‘3 step work test’ is that in our business you can do whatever work you want as long as you can do it –

Faster than a computer (i.e. 1 second);

Cheaper than an Indian (i.e. $5);

For at least 35 hours a day (i.e. the 35 in 1/3/35).

In other words, due to automation, outsourcing and accessing multiple time zones at once, we must focus on the areas where we add the most amount of value.

1/5/35

“Only as good as the next job”

While this is often used as a sports catch phrase, it is arguably derived from farming and gardening – i.e. it does not matter how well you have performed on a farm in a previous year – it is irrelevant if that same level of performance (or even better) is not attained in the following year.

“AAR”

AAR stands for after action review. It is a critical KPI for our business and has been inspired by both VeraSage and the military. It is a without fault review for the purposes of capturing our intellectual property and improving in the future.

“Honour those absent”

Talking about people, whether they are members of our team, customers or anyone else behind their back, in a way that does not honour their presence is a cancerous activity.

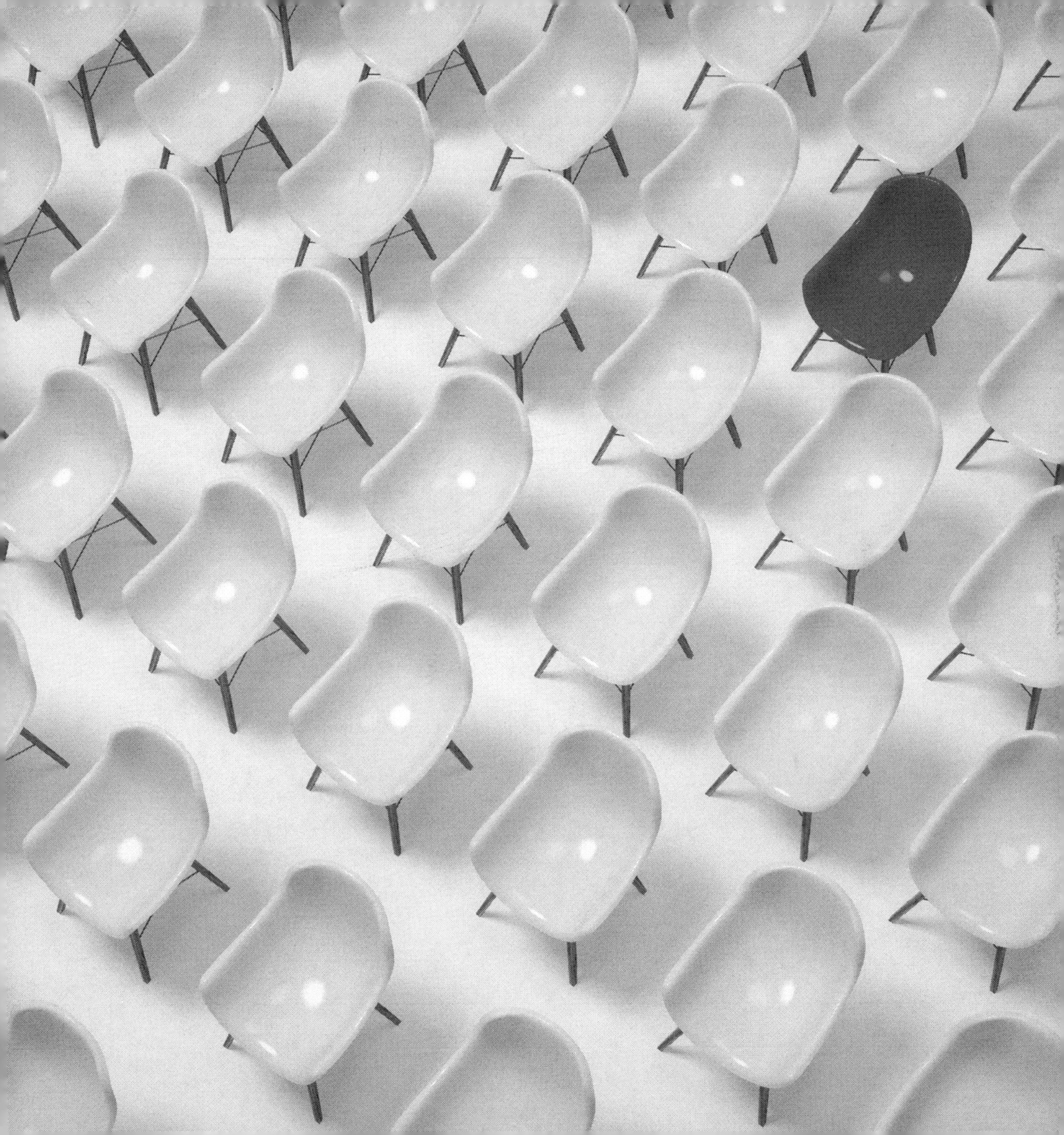

“Start with why”

Most people and organisations start by focusing on what they do and leave their why to the very end of their thinking – or perhaps never get to it.

‘Why’ is in fact where we all need to start, and invariably, it is not a why focused on ourselves, rather a why focused on how other people feel and interact with the solutions that we provide.

“7 Habits of Highly Effective People”

Essentially, every ‘self-help’ book is summarised into this one publication. It was ground breaking when released and remains almost without peer.

“Strengths focused activity leads to flow which leads to happiness ”

Common sense suggests that people should focus on their weaknesses to improve. Uncommon sense suggests that people should focus on their strengths.

“Apply uncommon sense”

Common sense is not in fact common.
Strive to apply uncommon sense.

LIBERTY
2003
D

“Every book we handout is a seedling for our next big job”

Books are still arguably the most sustaining and resonating form of marketing that there is. We have invested exceptionally heavily in our technical legal books, however for relatively nominal cost, we are able to have a permanent business card with everyone that we can legitimately sell or hand one to.

“Disruptive innovation is an undeniable truth”

Clayton Christensen has explained disruptive innovation for over two decades and our firm is founded in the belief that the legal industry is on the cusp of what has happened to countless other industries. We believe that if we are not disrupting our most profitable products with a cheaper, easier, IT driven solutions, then our competitors will be.

“Write a book”

There is a theory that every business founder should write at least one book explaining their vision.

“Remember from where we have come ”

Most, possibly all, ‘overnight success’ is the result of years of disciplined commitment.

Understanding this journey, particularly through story sharing, provides grounding for our success and inspires us to strive for the next step.

“What is the next step?”

One of the biggest causes of problems such as Parkinson’s Law is the inability to articulate the exact ‘next step’.

Simply defining the next step and agreeing who is accountable and by when can revolutionise a business.

"Have you checked (the back of) your iPhone"

Two sentences, on the back of every iPhone, explain value exceptionally well.

The two sentences are 'Designed in California. Assembled in China'.

“We grow with our customers”

A very significant proportion of our business is sourced from either repeat customers or direct personal referrals from previous customers. This is the sign of a truly fantastic business and something that we should never let go of.

“We are all predictably irrational”

Behavioural economics is a centrepiece of our business model.

?
1
2
yes
no
B

“Finish what you start”

Our ‘ping’ society sets us up for failure in terms of completing one task at a time. No person, regardless of their age or gender can multitask.

Finishing any task means not doing a single other task until the agreed job is entirely complete. No email checking. No phone calls. No social media. No grabbing a coffee. Do. What. Is. Needed. To. Ship.

“Just Ship It”

‘Shipping’ is the concept that our customers are only interested in the service being delivered to them – i.e. the product shipped. Embracing this mantra also means rejecting ideas such as time billing.

“We rage against the machine”

While the phase is perhaps best known as the name of the influential US rock band, our business is founded on not accepting the status quo (no band name pun intended).

“Find the choke point”

Like AAR’s (After Action Review), this is another concept borrowed from the military. Our business success depends on working out where the most important issues for our customers are – and then focusing our skills to create innovative fixes.

We similarly focus on solving the choke points in our own business.

TEMP
60
40
20
DEF

“More with less”

We define innovation in four words – doing more with less.

“Gamification”

A growing theory across all aspects of life, gamification focuses on making systems, services and activities more enjoyable and motivating.

“KISS is good”

‘Keeping it simple stupid’ is a fundamental concept that we benchmark back to wherever possible.

“B1G1”

B1G1 is the community focused charitable organisation that allows our business to regularly contribute to communities less fortunate than our own.

B1G1

“Entrepreneurship is not negotiable”

Our success is derived from entrepreneurial customers. We have no choice other than to be entrepreneurial ourselves.

“Equality of opportunity, not outcome”

All successful firms are based on the concept of giving everyone an opportunity, not guaranteeing some sort of equality of outcome.

“Differing views are fostered”

The different perspectives we all bring are critical to the ongoing growth and sustainability of our business.

“We only ever want one person accountable”

Organisations that start setting up committees for making decisions create inertia and bureaucracy that ultimately destroy the firm.

“Unconscious bias”

There are a vast array of common biases around concepts such as affinity bias, interest bias, pattern recognition and gender. We need to foster a culture to allow all of us to become self-aware.

“Technical excellence is simply the ticket to the event”

We, and in turn our customers, simply expect exceptional technical excellence. This is not a differentiator itself, however it means that we must all commit to significant professional development each and every week.

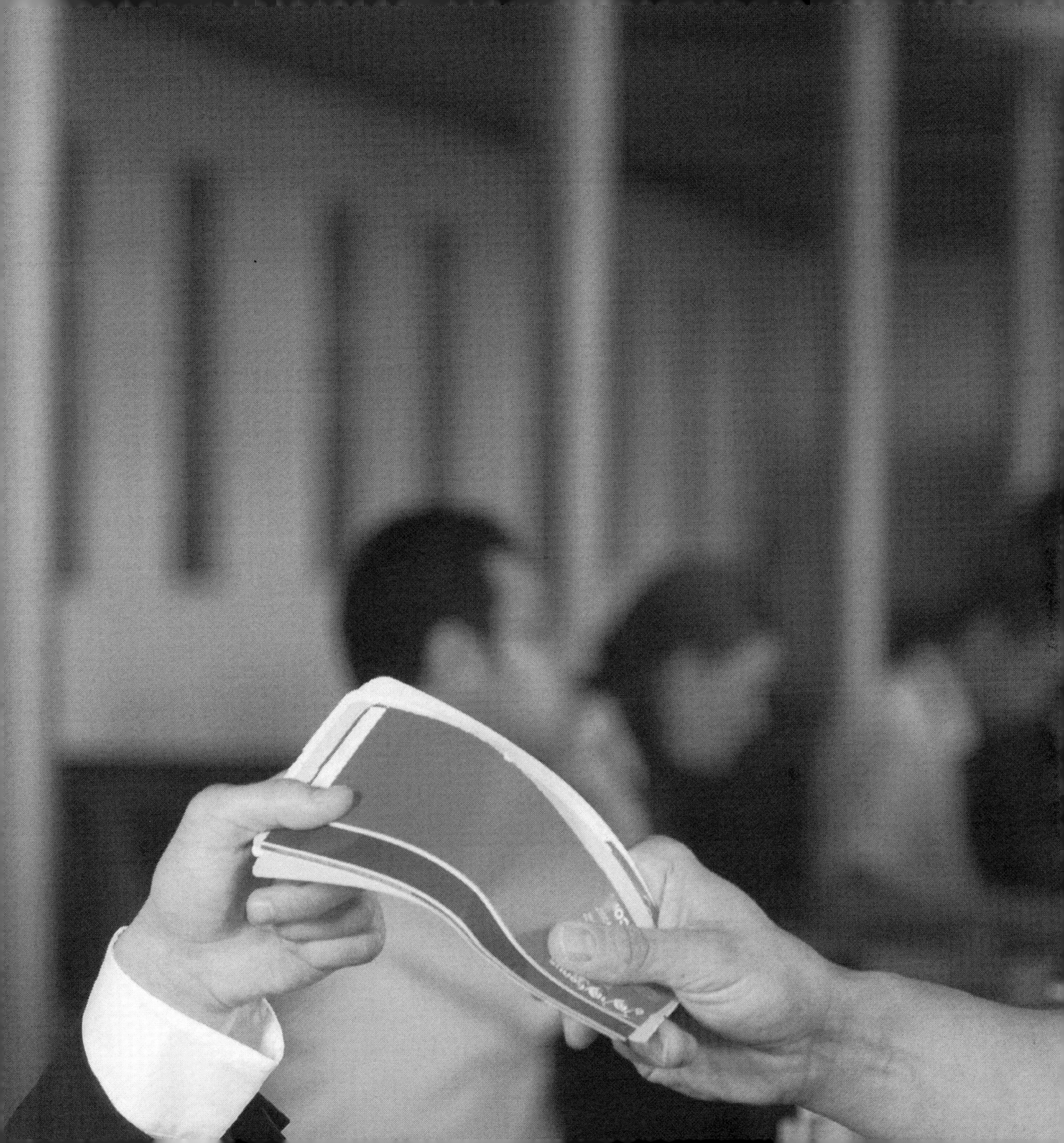

“Everything needs to be four-eyed”

Risks both in terms of technical content and commercial aspects can only be addressed where a second person reviews what you do. Take every available opportunity to have another review what you do and build the systems and processes to make them feel as though they are out of the job (i.e. they rarely ever find corrections).

“Print anything that is even remotely important”

It is impossible to see errors and problems on an electronic screen. Anything of importance should be printed and methodically read on hardcopy.

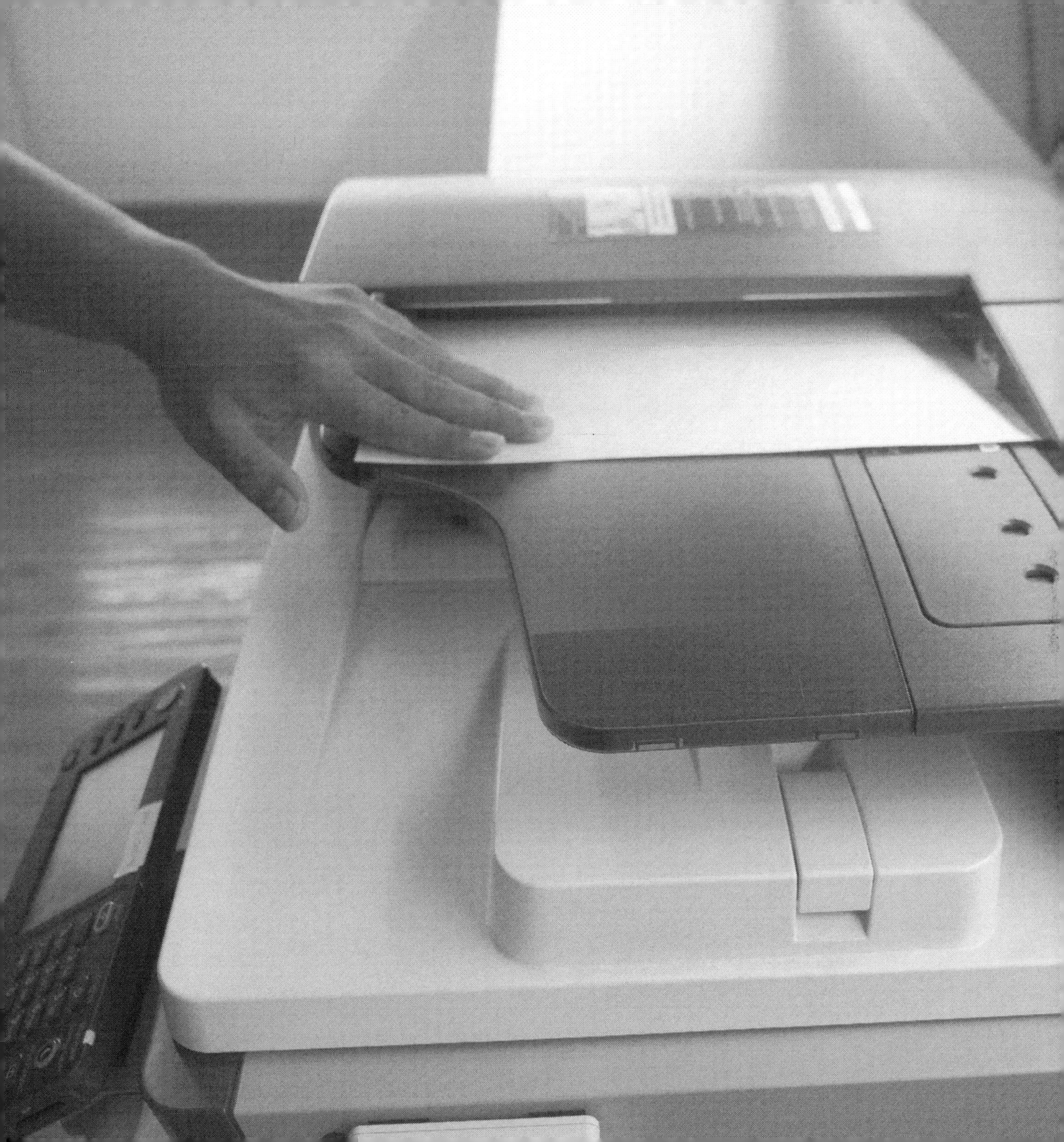

“Problem shared is a problem halved”

Whenever there is anything that is troubling you, find the way to share the issue. It is rare that someone else in our firm will not have had to worry about the same thing before. Even where there is no internal knowledge, invariably someone will have a lead to contacts outside the firm that can help.

“Our success depends on IP centralisation”

The ongoing disruptive nature of our business means that unless we can centralise and systemise everything that we do to ultimately automate it, we will not survive. It is imperative for all of us to take the extra time at the end of any task that might possibly be performed again to centralise that IP and to continue to build our precedents and knowledge bank.

“Confidentiality is non-negotiable ”

It is absolutely critical that we maintain complete confidentiality in relation to all customer related aspects of our business. It is impossible to over emphasise the importance of confidentiality and the concept should be considered in the widest possible terms even to the extent of sharing information internally within the firm about particular customer scenarios.

PRIVATE & CONFIDENTIAL

“We are part of a professional community”

We have a fantastic network of other advisers who we can leverage off whenever needed. If something is too hard, again we should look to reach out to these advisers.

“It’s not meant to be hard”

We have a standing mantra to test why something is getting bogged down. Great solutions are regularly provided by intelligent workarounds.

“Is there another way? ”

Adjacent to the ‘it’s not meant to be hard’ mantra is the mantra ‘is there another way? Invariably, the newest members of our firm are the ones best able to help with this goal.

P
DETOUR
YIELD
EXIT 6
ROAD SIGNS
NEXT EXIT
STOP
DETOUR
NO
PARKING
ANY
TIME
ROUTE
US
66
ROAD
WORK
AHEAD
DEAD
END
SPEED
LIMIT
55
TOW AWAY
ZONE
UNDER
CONSTRUCTION
DO NOT
ENTER
CONSTRUCTION
ZONE
INTERSTATE
95
R R
WRONG
WAY
ONE WAY

“1969 is the answer”

Any feedback, particularly in the technology space, along the lines of - ‘oh that can’t be done’, will generally be met with ‘1969’ as the response. In other words, given humans landed on the moon in 1969, there is nothing modern technology can not do.

“If you think of it, it exists”

The reality with our world is that if you can think of it, it either already exists; or will shortly.

Google
Google Search
I'm Feeling Lucky

“You’re the voice”

Our vocal health and delivery goes to the heart of our message.

We invest heavily in vocal training.

“Ass U me”

When we assume something to be the case it makes an ‘ass of you and me’.

“You are what you eat”

Physical health begins and ends with food choices.

We choose to eat real food, including starting each day with the now ubiquitous green smoothie.

“Every night is opening night”

Similar, yet different, to the concept of only being as good as your next job. The key here is understanding that in every situation you are on show, even if you may have performed the ‘same’ content countless times before.

“Dress to impress”

We embrace Richard Branson’s ‘Bye to the Tie’.

We also understand that ideally in any environment it is preferable to have a dress standard comparable to the best dressed in the room.

“IP is meant to be free”

Intellectual property, in the digital age, is meant to be freely available. We embrace this across all aspects of our business, with our articles, books, podcast channel, smart phone and tablet apps, webinars and seminars a few examples.

FREE

“There is no such thing as work-life balance”

The concept of trying to balance work and life as if they are separate concepts is nonsense.

We embrace roles and opportunities in a way that allows people to play to their strengths and achieve a satisfying level of integration between what they do get paid for and the parts of their life where they are not getting paid.

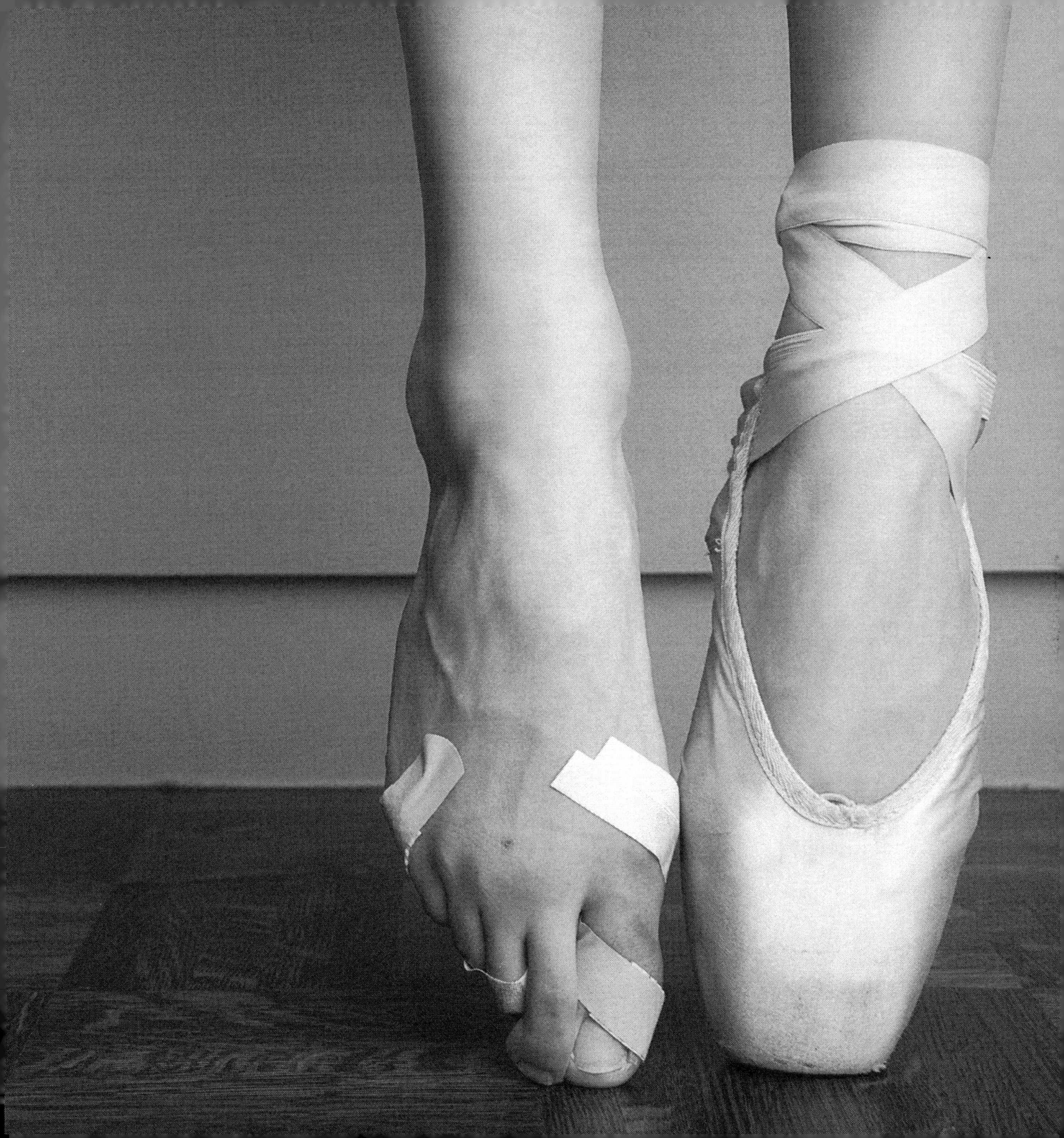

“ROWE ”

We are a ‘results only work environment’ – not interested in form filling performance reviews or completing timesheets to prove how ‘hard’ we might have worked. The product of our application is the only criteria that we measure.

> **“We spend equal time working on the business as in the business”**

We embrace the fact that our firm is a business and that it is critical to have key members ‘off the legal tools’ and thinking about how to be more relevant to our customers.

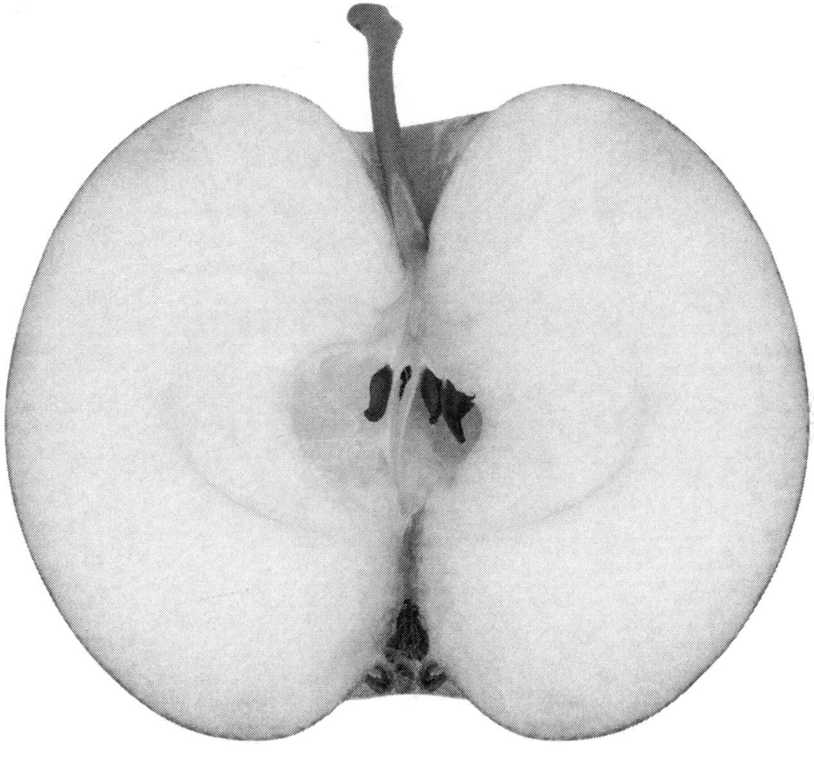

“Triple F”

We believe that the work environment should be flexible and fun and create flow. It is the responsibility of each person to take personal ownership of achieving this outcome each and every day. If there are people that you work with that you believe are preventing you attaining this outcome, raise it with them directly, and immediately (i.e. same day) when the issue arises.

“And; not or”

Historically businesses have focused on making ‘or decisions’ – i.e. doing one thing and not doing the other. Modern businesses need to find ways to embrace ‘and’. Our business has done that by (for example) embracing both high-end quality specialist advice and our online delivery solutions.

And; not or

“WWW”

Finish every day sharing with someone important to you ‘what went well’ that day personally and work wise.

ABC
education
Back to School

“MVP is key (the 1/1/90 rule)”

Getting a minimal viable product out into the market is the only way to test an idea. If you are not embarrassed by what is released, then you have released too late. We achieve this by having a priority (ie 1 of 1) goal, with 1 person accountable, that is shipped within 90 days.

1/1/90

“Healthy brains are carried by healthy bodies”

It is impossible to deliver in our space unless all physical and mental health is A grade. Exercise and eating real food (i.e. nothing processed) sets you up for success.

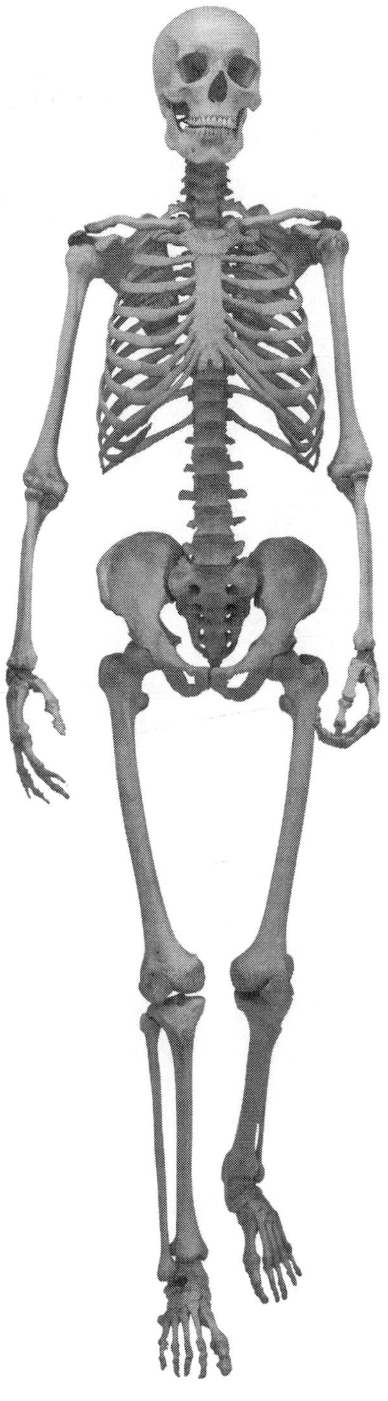

“Move everyday”

We have embraced concepts such as a stand-up desk and walking machines at work since the mid-2000s. Do whatever it takes to ensure that you are not sitting down for any extended periods, even in customer meetings.

1300 LIT SUP (548 787) litsupport.com.au
litsupport
job well done
Reliable. Dependable. Invested
PHILIPS

“Micro mentoring ”

We invest heavily in sharing and helping each of us achieve the key habits for success. We are not interested in constant check-ins about how workflow is progressing – we expect each person to be accountable for their business with the ultimate goal that each team member is tooled as quickly as possible to be in a situation where they could in fact establish their own business successfully.

“Hang out with five people each day that are better than you”

Your success will be determined by the people that you spend time with, even if it is simply by reading books by legendary thinkers. Make the effort every day to ensure that you have learnt something from at least five people smarter than you.

“Manage your energy, not your time”

Particularly with your hardest jobs, ensure that your energy levels are appropriate to allow completion.

“Diminishing returns”

With every task, there is a point where after deliberate and considerate investment; your learning will start to significantly drop off. Be alive to this concept on every job and share a problem or roadblock as soon as the diminishing returns start setting in.

94.51
News
1D 5D 1M 3M 1Y 3Y MAX
525.51
Volume

“We are still passionate about time”

While we do not track time spent on a task, we religiously track time to shipping – i.e. the duration that it has taken between receipt of instructions and delivery of end product.

16 JEWELS
0,2 S

“Make time for thinking”

Some form of meditation style thinking is required every day. If you are not into formal meditation, find a substitute – for example, the moving meditation offered by swimming.

“Routine is everything”

Having a disciplined routine frees up brain space and creates habits. Most successful people have exceptionally disciplined routines that they follow at all times, including down to wearing the exact same clothes every day.

"McDonald's marketing"

Our business is founded on the original McDonald's model (not the iteration that it has now become) – i.e. delivering one core product and being super famous for it. On the back of that product, we then upsell immediately adjacent products. For McDonald's, that was the basic range of hamburgers and then upselling into a soft drink, fries and dessert. For us, our core product is our estate planning solution and then our adjacent products are the tax planning, asset protection, structuring etc.

НАТАЛЬЯ
КАРТОФЕЛЬ ФРИ ОБЪЕДИНЯЕТ

“Zero inbox”

Each day should finish with there being zero items in the inbox. This is a big risk issue. If necessary, a separate ‘to-do’ or ‘action’ folder should be used.

0

“Leverage the team to manage emails”

All emails should be typed directly into your drafts folder by a typing team. Once you have settled them, the email should be separately moved into an ‘emails for sending’ folder and your admin team should send these.

“Be vigilant with equipment and material”

There are countless horror stories of, for example, children getting a hold of electronic equipment or staff accidentally leaving material somewhere that have caused significant damage to customers and business. Be vigilant and methodical in your safeguards in this area.

“Thinking that got us here won’t get us there”

The ideas and solutions that have worked in the past for historical problems are unlikely to be of use for new problems.

“The world is flat ”

The start of the end of many industries (including ‘Big Law’) was arguably back in the 1990s when the concept of global a workforce first materialised. We are constantly looking to embrace this framework still many years later.

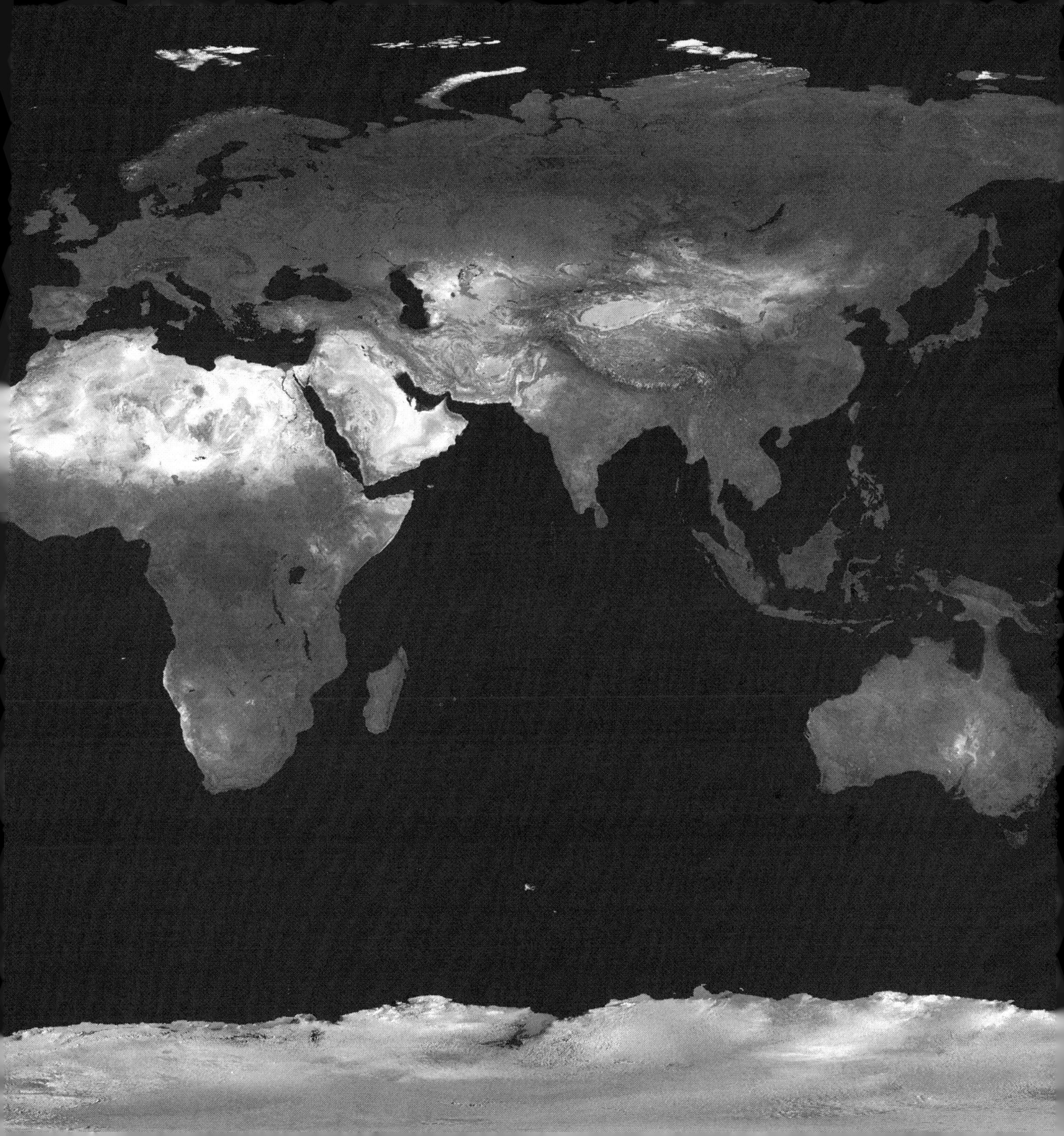

“Think fast and slow”

The literature in relation to the way our brains work and the seminal work ‘Thinking Fast and Slow’ is critical to understand in relation to our customers and also ourselves.

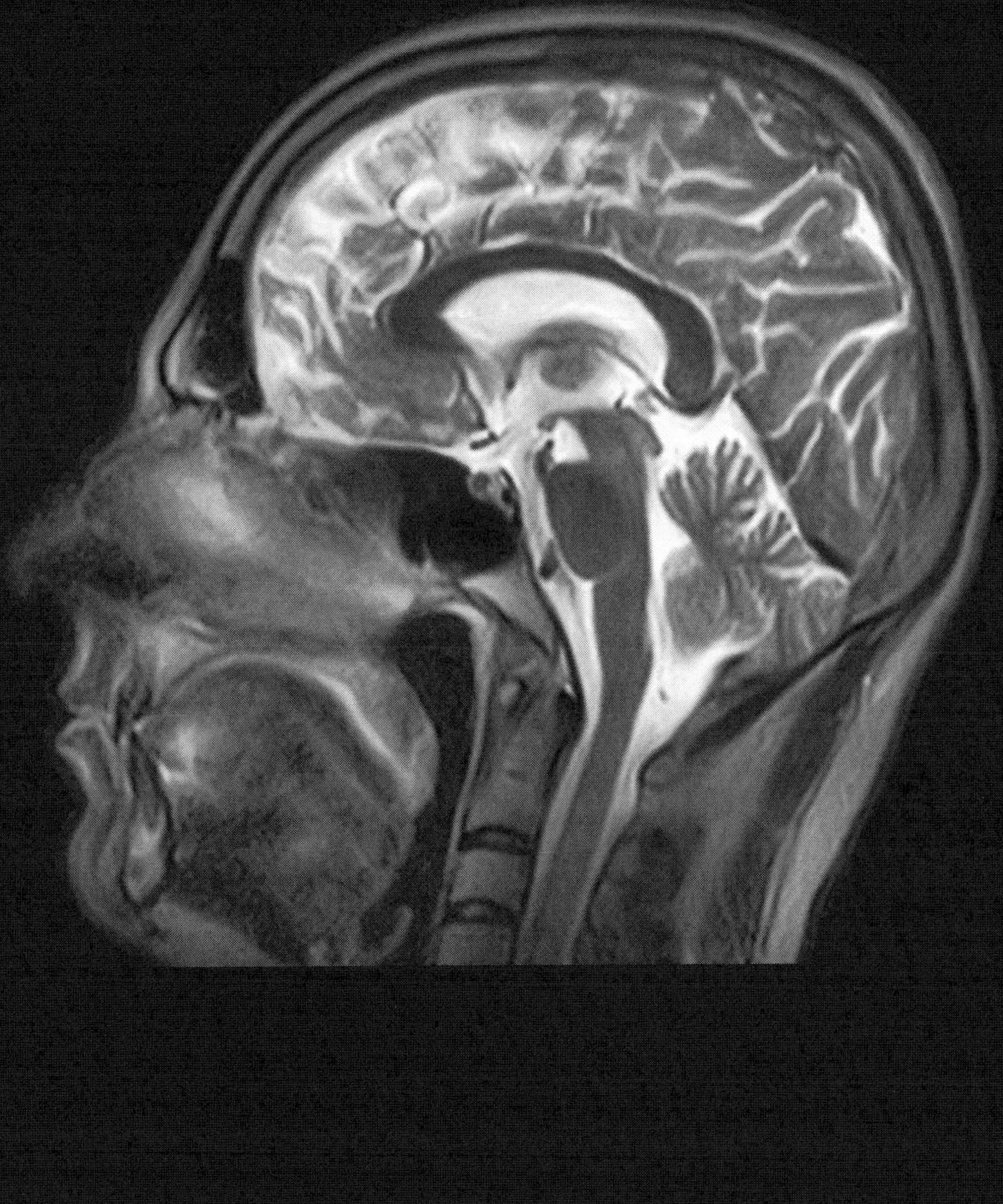

“Stay young, stay foolish ”

As mentioned in the foreword, this idea is derived from a quote often used by Steve Jobs, being to ‘stay hungry, stay foolish.’ The concept is that (similar to the mantra that ‘only the paranoid survive’) unless you are constantly enthusiastic for the future and keep your mind ‘child like’ in terms of being open to new ideas, you will be unsuccessful.

“Everything is borrowed”

The classic quote is that ‘good artists borrow, great artists steal.’

We embrace this mantra.

“We have no customers ”

We pride ourselves on being solely ‘business to business’ in our value proposition. This means that we never really have any customers at all – we treat our referral sources as if they were customers in a marketing sense. This also explains why we virtually never make referrals to other professionals – e.g. if an accountant refers a customer to us, no one will be interested in us then trying to refer that customer to a different accountant.

“Sanity is preserved via version control ”

Being methodical with version control goes to the heart of our business. This means that with any document that is being amended, it is vital to save it into a new version, accept any existing redline and then always amend in redline.

“Fail fast”

All leading firms find a way to get products to market quickly, make the errors that are always made, then even more rapidly fix those errors and iterate the product so that it is attractive to a customer. Some argue the difference between success and failure can largely be determined by the time delays between conceptualising a product or improvement and getting that product or improvement into the market.

7
5

“We double our chances of having great team members with one simple strategy”

We believe talent is not determined by gender; unlike the vast majority of law firms that are lucky to have a double-digit percentage of female leaders.

“21 tips for young players”

There is a famous list of 21 ideas for success by H Jackson Brown that is always a timely reminder.

“Brain food”

Piecing together a summary of the most influential books and articles you read is a key to success.

“Checklists are everything ”

A lot of our thinking behind the importance of checklists is set out in our ‘checklist manifesto platform’. There is also an amazing amount of literature around two quite starkly different treks to the summit of Everest some years ago. The leader of one trek tragically perished, along with the majority of his group. The other group that suffered no casualties built their entire operation around checklists.

CHECKLIST

“Get a coin toss app”

With reference to some of the ideas in this book (including Thinking Fast and Slow), often the most important thing to do is to make a decision, rather than what the decision itself might be. A coin toss app helps solve many a dilemma. Use it earlier, use it often.

“When in doubt, flick it out ”

With anything that you are considering the usefulness of delegating it or referring it, if you have to stop and think about whether it is the appropriate thing to do, then you are in doubt, and you should therefore flick it out.

“We want our entire business runnable via our iPhones ”

Mobile is it. We need to find a way to ensure that every aspect of our business embraces a mobile centric solution.

“Know your phone”

Knowing as much about what your phone can do to leverage our business is the starting point.

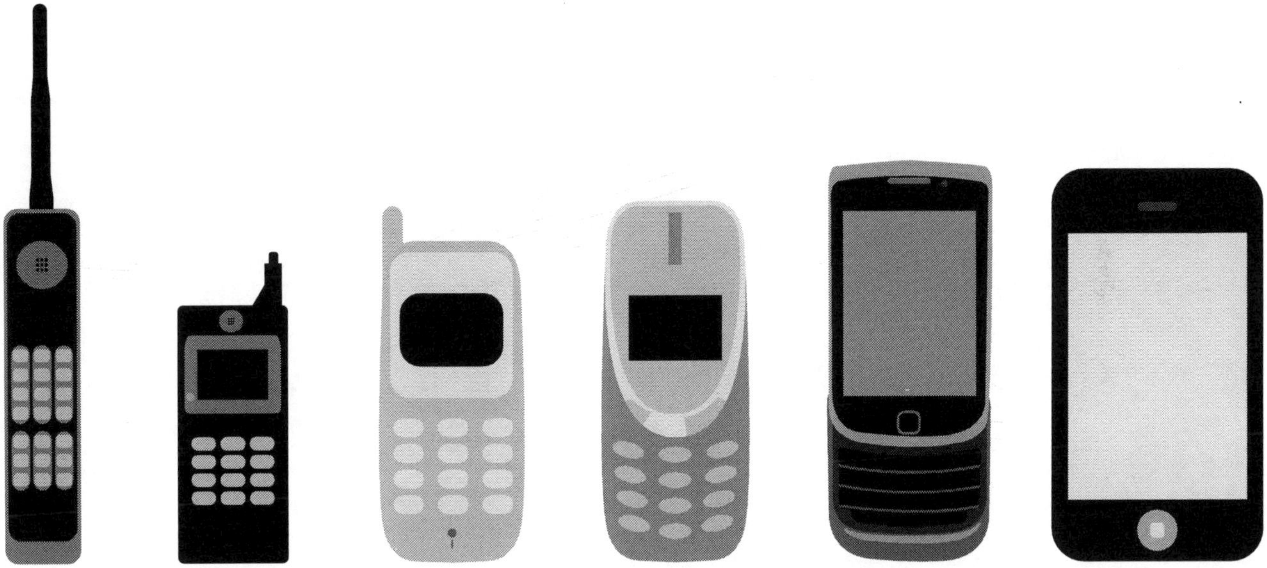

“There is an app for that ”

Almost every issue we face has a solution of some description (often a near perfect answer) via a smart phone app.

Unlock
Lock

“AI is here”

Artificial Intelligence is rapidly becoming ubiquitous across all aspects of life.
The provision of legal solutions will be drastically and irrecoverably changed by AI.

We can ‘get on and hang on’ or choose some other game to play.

“Rule of 7/11/4”

This used to be the rule of 7 – i.e. it previously took 7 forms of interaction in a marketing sense for a referral source to be convinced to try us out. The number is now more like 7 hours of content, on 11 separate occasions, across 4 mediums. The trick is we never really will understand what things actually constitute a true interaction nor what referral sources place more emphasis on – hence our extremely broad and agnostic approach to all things marketing.

7/11/4

“Strategy is about no”

True strategy is about saying no to things that are not completely aligned with where you are trying to get to.

“You only die once … ”

… so make sure it is worth it.

Acknowledgement

This book is the result of contributions from a number of people, each of whom I thank.

More particularly:

(1) All of the clients I have been fortunate enough to assist over the years have had significant influence on me personally, and obviously, the stories of a number of them form the foundation of this book.

(2) While I only know a handful of the people quoted personally, all of them also have had a significant influence on me, and again obviously, this book.

(3) There have been countless people involved, as with any book production, in reviewing, editing, designing and ultimately publishing it. The contribution of each and every person is very gratefully acknowledged.

(4) The team of people that I work with at View Legal have inspired me virtually every day for many years now. Personal thanks to the entire team.

(5) Finally, very deep and personal thanks to my family, and in particular, my immediate family. This book is the only tangible thing to show for countless weeks I have spent away from them reading, researching, collating and writing. It also signifies the end, at least for the time being, of a project that in its current form has been around one year of focused effort and energy.

Interested to learn more?

View has invested heavily to help advisers help their clients.

Some popular examples of adviser tools are as follows:

1. Subscribe to the free weekly blog posts:

http://blog.viewlegal.com.au/?m=1

To subscribe to the blog, simply enter your email address in the subscription box in the right hand column or alternatively, subscribe through your preferred RSS feed from your browser.

2. View Intellectual Property platform (VIP)

The VIP subscription platform provides you with free access to our webinars, as well as preferred pricing to our books, entity establishment, superannuation and estate planning solutions.

Even if you trial the VIP platform to update your own estate planning and structuring arrangements it represents fantastic value.

Learn more at—

http://viewlegal.com.au/view-vip-subscription-platform-2/

3. Education programs

View Legal specialises in all forms of adviser education and collaborative learning.

We are fortunate to regularly present to accountants, financial planners, other lawyers and risk advisers.

Our programs are tailored to meet your specific requirements and can be delivered in lengths ranging from 20 minute web-based updates to 5 day in-house courses (and every permutation in between) and formats including in person, webinar and video streaming. Our most popular sessions tend to be 90 minute team trainings, which can be recorded for future use.

A sample of some of our current topics is set out at the following link—

http://viewlegal.com.au/product-category/events/

Or simply stream or purchase DVD copies of previous programs via the following link—

http://viewlegal.com.au/recorded-webinars/

4. Business model iteration

Matthew Burgess has been recognised as a thought leader in delivery of professional service solutions by peers, industry commentators and competitors. He regularly presents keynotes in this area as well as coordinating and facilitating firm retreats and education programs.

Indeed, Matthew is the only practising lawyer in Australia who is a Certified Speaking Professional (CSP), a designation conferred by the Professional Speakers Australia (PSA), the industry's leading organisation. The CSP is likewise the speaking profession's international measure of professional platform competence.

Matthew is counted among the rare 12 percent of professional speakers worldwide who currently hold the CSP credential.

Learn more about Matthew's business model presentations here—

https://viewlegal.com.au/matthewburgessspeaking/

Learn more about the business books Matthew has written here—

http://www.thedreamenabler.com.au/

A Selection of Other Books from View Legal

For all the latest books please visit *https://viewlegal.com.au/product-category/books/*

About View

At View Legal our mantra is to be 'for friends'.

In other words, creating solutions and value propositions that are compelling to our friends.

To achieve our vision, we have set out to fundamentally and radically revolutionise access to high quality legal advice, in our areas of deep specialisation—structuring, tax, trusts, asset protection, business sales, estate and succession planning.

To help explain the approach View is taking to uniquely deliver valuable legal solutions, the following table lists 10 traditional ways law firms have operated (and, almost exclusively, continue to operate) and the new vision that View is built around.

Old view	View Legal
Bill clients on hourly rates (or various, increasingly elaborate, permutations on the theme) and have no particular interest in client perception of value	Customers provided up front 'SPS Guarantee'—that is service and price satisfaction is guaranteed with all work undertaken following upfront fixed pricing
Everything tracked on a timesheet. The longer something takes, the better	No timesheets. Sophisticated project management tools used to help ensure customer expectations are exceeded
Quality is defined by the law firm	Quality is defined by the customer
'Impressive' CBD office space, with 'dominant' fit outs	View meets where best suits customers. No permanent CBD space retained
Intellectual property is how we make money and should be guarded jealously	Intellectual property is how we create trust and should be shared freely
Lawyers striving to deliver near-perfect technical excellence	All service designed to be fit-for-purpose, aligning with collaboratively agreed customer objectives
Lawyers cultural focus on 'is this billable' for the firm	Lawyers cultural focus on 'is this valuable' for the customer
'Leveraging' of full-time lawyers to do the bulk of the work serving clients	Flexible work practices that match supply with demand
Constant focus on the 'need for diversity' of gender	Only focus on diversity of thought
Revenue growth the #1 goal	Exceeding customer expectations #1 goal

Significant inspiration provided by VeraSage. Partly adapted with permission of George Beaton, Beaton Capital.

If you would like to learn more about any of the above solutions or View more generally contact 1300 View 00 (1300 843 900), email mail@viewlegal.com.au or contact one of the founders listed at the foot of our home page at—*http://viewlegal.com.au/*

About the Author

Matthew Burgess is one of the founders of specialist firm View Legal.

Having the opportunity to help clients achieve their goals is what he is most passionate about.

As Matthew always works in conjunction with trusted advisers (whether it be accountants, financial advisers or other lawyers) and their clients, finding ways to fundamentally improve the value received by those advisers, and in turn their clients, has led him to develop numerous game changing models. Examples include providing guaranteed upfront fixed pricing, founding what is widely regarded as Australia's first virtual law firm, and more recently, developing a platform that gives advisers access to market leading advice and support for less than $1 a week.

Matthew's specialisation in tax, structuring, asset protection, estate and succession planning has seen him recognised by most leading industry associations including the Tax Institute, the Weekly Tax Bulletin and in the 2014 'Best Lawyers' list for trusts and estates and either personally, or as part of View, since 2015 in 'Doyles' for taxation and since 2017 for wills, estates and succession planning.

Work is one aspect of his life Matthew loves, so there is no need to be constantly searching for 'balance'. His other great loves are:

1. Family—they are profiled in various ways through the series of children's books he has written under the pseudonym 'Lily Burgess'—see *www.wordsfromdaddysmouth.com.au* and various TV commercials;
2. Learning—going cold Turkey on television and most forms of media in late 2005 has radically increased Matthew's ability to study the great authors and inspired him to publish a series of books that explore the concept of 'true success'—see *www.thedreamenabler.com.au*
3. Health—aside from being a foodie and swimming at least 5km a week, Matthew installed a stand up workstation in 2007 and among a few other lifestyle choices, it changed his life.

Testimonials

A selection of testimonials for presentations by View (including for organisations such as The Tax Institute, various law societies, Television Education Network, AMP, NAB and ALPMA) are as follows:

> Excellent session. Full of interactivity and practical examples/cases.
>
> I wanted to send you a quick note to say that I thought the session you presented was superb and certainly in my top 2 for the entire event.
>
> Your session was the one that we were able to take away the most useful information. We managed to totally can our latest project and built a new one by the time we hit the airport to head home!
>
> Thank you for your excellent presentation at the conference today. In a sentence, it was very inspiring.
>
> Your session was unreal. Very engaging, honest and fun.
>
> Your presentation was simply fantastic! A lesson in how to take the dull and boring and make it fun and entertaining.

100%
YOU
London
Paris
Berlin
Moscow
Beijing
Tokyo
Sydney
Los Angeles
New York
1/5/35
B1G1
Google
FREE
And; not or
1/1/90
7/11/4

Made in United States
Orlando, FL
04 November 2026

90202231R00120